SUCCESS: WHY YOU FAIL WHERE OTHERS SUCCEED

5 LIFE-CHANGING PERSONAL DEVELOPMENT TIPS YOU WISH YOU KNEW

THIBAUT MEURISSE

© 2016 Thibaut Meurisse

All rights reserved. No portion of this book may be reproduced in any form without permission from the publisher, except as permitted by U.S. copyright law.

CONTENTS

Foreword   v

1. You Shall Not Mistake «Your Reality» For Reality   1
2. You shall Not Let Your Thoughts Define Who You Are   20
3. You Shall Be Clear on the Meaning of Success   27
4. You Shall Be the Creator of Your Life   31
5. You Shall Set Goals   45
   Conclusion   54

Would you like to set and achieve exciting goals?   55
What do you think?   57
Other Books By The Authors: 59
About the Author   61
Need Some Help to Achieve Your Goals?   63

FOREWORD

I would like to thank you for downloading this e-book. I hope it will become a valuable tool for your personal growth.

In this book, rather than giving you simple tips to improve your life I will provide you with several key concepts that I believe you absolutely need to understand and master in order to fully reach your potential and attain the level of fulfillment you truly deserve in life. These principles are the foundation on which you should base your personal development work. They will require that you work on yourself before you master them but I assure you that the investment of time and effort is well worth it. As Jim Rohn said *'Learn to work harder on yourself than you do on your job. If you work hard on your job you will make a living, if you work hard on yourself you can make a fortune."* The time to work hard on yourself is NOW!

Let's get started.

1
YOU SHALL NOT MISTAKE «YOUR REALITY» FOR REALITY

> *A human being always acts and feels and performs in accordance with that he imagines to be true about himself and his environment.*
>
> — MAXWELL MALTZ, PSYCHO-CYBERNETICS

Our vision of life is nothing more than a constructed reality. We weren't born with limitations on what we can or cannot do. Those limitations were artificially created afterwards. What your current mindset and way of thinking identifies as impossible could very well sound perfectly achievable for someone else with more empowering thoughts.

Have you ever noticed how babies have almost an unlimited potential to grow and learn? It is simply because they intuitively trust their brain which allows them to make full use of their potential. They don't place artificial limitations of what they can and can't do.

The human brain is an extraordinarily powerful machine but, unfortunately, most people don't know how to use it properly. The reason why our subconscious mind is so powerful is because it is a mechanical goal-seeking device. It works through trial and error and will make all the adjustments needed over time until it reaches the goal it was programmed to achieve. The truth is that our mind needs failure! No great inventions would have come into existence without failure. Remember Thomas Edison's "failures." He didn't define them as failures but rather he said *"I have not failed. I've just found 10,000 ways that won't work."*

One reason why many people fail to use the full power of their mind is simply because they forget to apply this trial and error process in order to move forward with their life. In other words, they are afraid to fail and because of that they never make the mistakes that our brain desperately needs in order to achieve our goals. Another critical reason is that they have limiting beliefs—artificial limitations existing only in their mind and created through their interpretation of past events. Phobias and fear of abandonment are both strong examples of limiting beliefs.

We all have different perceptions of the world that resulted from our past experiences and the way we chose to react consciously or unconsciously to those past events. For that reason, what I think is possible might be different from what you think is possible. Have you ever heard someone tell you to *be realistic*? Or have you ever told someone to *be realistic*? If you analyze this expression closely you realize that it is entirely subjective. What people are telling you is simply *"What you are trying to accomplish is not aligned with 'my reality' based on what I conceive as possible through the belief system I'm currently operating upon."* However their reality is not your reality!

Our reality is in fact based on our personal interpretation of the world and what we choose to focus on constantly. Our current reality is not the result of our past experience. It is the result of our personal interpretation of past experiences in addition to specific parts of reality that we choose to focus our attention on.

Your reality is not the true reality because:

- You are operating under a belief system that is the result of your personal interpretation of past events. Your beliefs determine your actions and prevent you from realizing your potential.
- You can only grasp a tiny part of reality and it's the part you choose to focus your attention on.

Now let's see how you can create a more empowering reality by:

- Becoming more optimistic
- Identifying your limiting beliefs and deconstructing them

How to become optimistic

Do you know what the difference between pessimistic and optimistic people is? It's simply their focus. In your daily life, you can always identify an infinite number of negative things, but you can also identify an unlimited number of positive things. Being pessimistic or being optimistic is a choice. Every day we are creating our reality by choosing what to focus on.

In reality, pessimism is of very little use. How does it help you improve your life? It is absolutely critical that you work on being more optimistic and have a positive outlook on life. Negative thoughts are harming your mental health and limiting your potential. They don't help you get the life you deserve. Now, being optimistic doesn't mean denying reality! It just means making a *conscious* choice to focus on the positive side of life and, while acknowledging the reality of unpleasant facts, choosing not to spend time or energy focusing on them. It is a perfectly rational behavior! Actually, any time spent worrying is irrational. It is important for you to understand this and do what you can to worry less.

Actually, we have a strong bias towards negativity. We are more sensitive to unpleasant events than we are to pleasant events. In the past, it was critical for our survival that our brain notice every possible kind of danger that could threaten our life. That's why we are so sensitive to negative events. However nowadays it's useless 99% of the time. Why should you worry about a future that doesn't exist? Why should you worry about a past that is no more? Why complain about what is happening to you right now. Reality is. That's it!

Studies show that the ratio between the amount of positive and negative interactions between a married couple can predict their likeliness of divorce. To ensure a healthy relationship, this ratio must be at least 5:1.

The bottom line is that we already have a strong negative bias. Thus, it is important that we make an effort to focus on positive things in our life to offset that bias and maintain our inner peace.

What about you? Do you see the glass as half full or half empty? Why not retrain yourself to become more optimistic? That is exactly what I did.

Here is what you can do to become more optimistic:

Stop watching TV

Jim Rohn once wisely observed that *"Poor people have a big TV. Rich people have a big library."* TV can certainly be entertaining but it won't help you grow. The real wealth of knowledge is accessible in books and in your real life—not on TV. Be aware of this, it's important. Why not challenge yourself to stop watching TV for a week or a month and see how you like it?

Still not convinced? Here are some good reasons to stop watching TV:

It manipulates your emotions

Kelly McGonigal in her book "The Willpower Instinct" wrote: "Studies show that being reminded of our mortality makes us more susceptible to all sorts of temptations, as we look for hope and security in the things that promise reward and relief." Another study demonstrated that we react more positively to advertisements for status products like luxury cars and watches when exposed to reports of death on the news. We unconsciously try to find comfort and safety by buying things. Were you aware of how advertisers manipulate your emotions?

It steals your time

It is easier to watch TV than to do many other activities but does watching TV leave you with a sense of fulfillment at the end of the day? Could you use your time for something else that is more important or productive?

It dictates to you what to think

TV and other forms of media subtly form opinions *for you*—what color of clothes you should wear this spring, how to behave, how much income to earn and even your definition of success and happiness. It is an impediment to personal growth. It robs you of your ability to think clearly and independently.

It distorts reality

For obvious reasons, there are more negative than positive things on TV. We generally don't talk about positive things because they don't scare well which means they don't sell well. The vast majority of folks are getting just fine? *Boring*! Let's create fear by talking about the latest terrorist threat, robbery or tragedy. TV gives you the illusion that the world is headed for disaster. I have a friend who is constantly complaining about politics and economics, he's always going off about how the experts on TV are all idiots. Recently he was warning me that the ebola virus was going to kill all of us. He is, perhaps as you may have guessed, also struggling in his personal and professional life—he's unhappy. I advise him to stop focusing on things he has no control over and focus on changing himself instead, by working on his attitude, his mindset and his skills. The truth is that you are not responsible for changing the world, you are only responsible for changing yourself. The more you work on yourself, the more you will be able to influence the world.

It prevents you from enjoying quality time with your family or friends

Are you watching TV during lunch or dinner at home? Watching TV with your family can be enjoyable but it can also rob you of more meaningful conversations with people you care about. When I came to Japan, I was surprised to see that many restaurants had TVs. You see customers watching TV rather than talking to each other.

Spend less time reading/watching the news

The news is way too negative and gives you a distorted view of reality. One tip: check the news weekly instead of daily in order to reduce your daily intake of negativity or read inspirational material/watch inspirational videos after reading/watching the news.

Spend less time with negative relatives or remove yourself from them

Do you have negative people around that criticize everything you do? Negative people can consume a lot of your energy and make it hard for you to maintain a positive outlook on life. According to Jim Rohn *"You are the average of the five people you spend the most time with."* You'd better choose them wisely.

Start your day by reading inspirational material or watching inspirational videos

Chicken Soup For The Soul by Jack Canfield is a good start. It is a collection of very short uplifting stories divided into several categories such as "on love," "learning to love yourself" or "live your dream." Many inspirational videos can be found on YouTube—check them out! Inspirational videos aren't everything, but if you listen to them daily they will help you stay motivated. Remember Zig Ziglar's words,

> *People often say that motivation doesn't last. Well, neither does bathing—that's why we recommend it daily.*

Use positive affirmations/visualization daily

Affirmations are words you repeat to yourself every day until they reach your subconscious mind. As you start to believe in those words, the way you feel and behave will change. Here is what you should consider when using positive affirmations:

Use the present tense and not the future tense ("I am" not "I will")
Avoid negative forms: don't say « I'm not shy » but "I'm confident"
Repeat the sentence for 5 minutes (use a timer for convenience)

Do it *every single day* without exception for at least a month, and preferably 2 months.

Note that when there is too much discrepancy between the positive affirmation you're saying to yourself and what you really believe about yourself, at the subconscious level, the affirmation might not work or it will take several months more before it works.

Here is how you can use positive affirmations efficiently:

1. Support your affirmations with real life experiences

For instance, just saying to yourself « I'm confident » won't work if deep down you don't believe it. However, if you ask yourself *Am I really not confident all the time and in every area of my life without exception?*—you will come up with things you feel confident doing. You will start realizing that your belief « I'm not confident » is not entirely true.

Questioning yourself is a powerful tool because you are no longer fighting against your subconscious mind by affirming things that it doesn't believe; you simply question your subconscious mind to see whether it misinterpreted reality. You start working hand in hand with your subconscious rather than fighting it. (See below "Deconstruct your limiting beliefs" for more information). Include things you are already confident about, regardless of how small they may be, and say to yourself *I'm confident because of ____ and ____*. You will find that it works better than simple affirmations.

2. While saying positive affirmations, visualize yourself embodying what you want to be

Your mind cannot tell the difference between something you simply imagined and an actual experience. If you want to be more confident visualize yourself being confident in the desired situation. You can imagine yourself being confident at a party or during a presentation for instance. By doing this you create new experiences. Because those experiences are interpreted as real, your subconscious mind won't stand in your way anymore. Build a reservoir of empowering "experiences" to bolster your confidence.

3. Add movements and emotions

Your words, your body and your thoughts are interconnected and influence each other. Using all three together is more powerful than simply using words.

4. Learn to reframe any situation by focusing on the positive

You can always find the positive in any situation and you should train yourself to do so. The more you practice this the more it will come naturally. Why waste your energy trying to deny reality wishing things were different? Yet this is exactly what most people do all the time and it's absurd!

Always accept reality. What *is* is so don't fight it! Why deny it? In fact, reality in and of itself is neutral. It is your interpretation of it that creates your problems. You are empowering your worst enemy, stop it! Eckhart Tolle wisely advised: *"Whatever the present moment contains, accept it as if you had chosen it."* Once you have accepted your situation focus on all the positive aspects you can think of. Ask yourself:

- *What can I do about it?*
- *How can I reframe the situation?*
- *What can I learn from this situation? How can it help me become a better person?*
- *Will I remember this in 20 years?*

When I went to Philippines in 2012, I was stuck on a small island unable to reach my final destination, Boracay, because of a flood. We were stuck in a hotel and didn't know when we would be able to finally reach Boracay. We planned to spend only 3 nights there and we had already missed one and it was looking like we may miss the remaining 2 nights. Let's try to apply the above framework:

What can I do about it? Nothing. Just wait for now.

How can I reframe the situation? It will make a great story to tell to my friends and it's the first time I've experienced a real flood. I can meet new people—that I otherwise wouldn't have been able to meet—here at the hotel and if we can reach Boracay tomorrow we will better enjoy our time there (knowing how precious the opportunity is).

What can I learn from this situation? How can it help me become a better person? I can feel proud of myself for staying calm and not wasting energy by needlessly panicking or complaining about a situation I can do nothing about.

Will I remember it in 20 years? Probably, but it won't be a bad memory at all!

Now we were able to reach the island the next morning and I actually enjoyed the short time I had there far more. Have you ever hiked a mountain? Have you noticed how good your simple meal tasted after a day of hiking? Nearly losing my trip and my positive reframing engineered gratitude that made the trip that much better. Start small by reframing mundane events that irritate you in your daily life. Soon you will become a master.

Remember that no situation has the power to make you miserable without your consent.

It is not the situation that matters, it is how you choose to react to it. Tip: Instead of seeing problems start seeing "challenges" or "opportunities." I try to never use the word "problem" because I believe it is not an empowering term. Reframe problems as challenges and failures as learning opportunities and big failure as massive learning opportunities! Lastly, ask yourself *"What can I learn from this situation that will help me to grow?"*

Our reality can only exist through our thoughts and what we choose to focus on. Our problems in life are only as big as we desire them to be. A problem, no matter how big it is for you right now, was created through the thoughts you are having about it and it will continue to exist as long as you commit time to thinking about it. If you were to never think again about that particular problem again, it would disappear. Why? Because your reality is always created by your own mind. If you don't think about something, for your mind it simply ceases to exist. Conversely, focusing on a problem, reinforces the connection in your brain between the problem and the emotional attached to it.

Now, I understand that in reality it is difficult to completely stop thinking about a problem that bothers you. Especially, because we have a strong tendency to compare ourselves to others which is *stupid*. However, you can make your problems smaller by spending less and less time thinking about them. If it is something you cannot change, you should definitely stop thinking about it right now. If you were born with no arms and no legs, there is no point wishing you had arms and legs as said by the motivational speaker Nick Vujicic who were born with no arms and no legs. Your problems are only as big as you want them to be. That's it! Now do you want larger or smaller problems?

Some of us have great difficulty getting rid of our problems because they've slowly become part of our identity, sometimes this occurs without us being consciously aware of it. If you are stuck where you are, it might be because you are buying into your current struggles or problems without necessarily being aware of it. I remembered how I use to take pleasure in having the problems I had a few months ago. Maybe you are proud of struggling with money or having low self-esteem? Are you getting addicted to your struggles and playing the role of the victim, or are you taking full responsibility for your life? You might enjoy the role of a victim without even being aware of it. You may enjoy the temporary attention that your "problems" generate from friends or family but it's an illusion that is keeping you mired in mediocrity. Try to catch yourself playing the victim. We all play this role at times and of course some more than others. It is time to stop playing the victim and re-empower yourself.

You are the victim only in your own mind.

Now, let's have a look at how your reality was actually created.

Your reality is defined by your belief system

Your belief system consist of all the beliefs that make up your subjective reality.

What is a belief? A belief is simply something that you accept as true, regardless of whether or not it actually is.

Where do your beliefs come from? Your beliefs come from the way you interpreted past events and are the result of:

- What you have heard (from your parents, your friends, your teachers, the media...)

- What you have experienced

- Positively: love from your parents, good results at school...
- Negatively: trauma (abuse, humiliation, failure...)

There are two ways your beliefs were created:

- Strong emotions
- Repetition

Strong emotions

A shocking event in your childhood sends a strong signal to your subconscious mind that it should protect you from experiencing similar events in the future. That's how phobias or fear of failure is created in the mind.

Repetition

Repetition is the key to create new beliefs and it is also how most of your current beliefs were created and often it's done unconsciously. Have you heard of religious cults where gurus have total control over the members? After repeating the same message again and again our subconscious mind actually starts to accept the message as true. People who join such cults are usually vulnerable and in search of a better reality than their current one. As a result, they are more likely to accept new beliefs as the truth. Propaganda is based on the same principle. We are weaker than we often think and can be easily influenced, whether we admit it to ourselves or not.

The bottom line is that, when we were young we accepted some limiting beliefs as reality without being consciously aware of it. It is not uncommon that a limiting belief you have came from your parents who possibility inherited it from their parents who inherited from their parents. Not only are some of your beliefs not yours but they are generations old! How many people suffer from a scarcity complex derived from the generation that survived the Great Depression?

Let me share with you one example given to me by my friend: "I used to use the same pot of coffee for days if not an entire week, to save what—30 cents? One day a friend of mine pointed this out as strange. I had no idea it was odd, because my father does that as well so I asked him why and he said his father did the same thing. During the 1930's nothing was wasted in order to survive, yet even though my father and myself are both perfectly capable of affording an extra coffee pot we are behaving as if we are in the midst of another great depression." Examine your own beliefs and behaviors and consider if they are still relevant to this age in history and to your own life.

Your subconscious mind is like big brother

Some limiting beliefs might prevent you from living the life you want. However, the first step is to understand that your subconscious mind means to do no harm to you. Your subconscious is always doing its best to protect you. Let's use phobia as an example. Phobias are the result of traumatic past experiences. Our subconscious mind associated a strong negative emotion to a particular situation. In order for that situation to never happen again, your subconscious mind creates a mechanism that keeps you away from similar situations that could endanger you.

So don't get angry at your subconscious mind but give the little guy some credit—he's trying to protect you. Collaborate with him and work at uncovering the root causes of your disempowering beliefs or phobias.

Your subconscious mind is in reality way more powerful than you can even begin to imagine. It regulates all of your bodily functions without you needing to be conscious of it. In addition to that, it acts in accordance with the beliefs you consciously or unconsciously accept as true. Ultimately, it controls most your life.

Why does it control your life? Because your belief system creates your thoughts, those thoughts create emotions and those emotions create behaviors. That's why profound changes are impossible without working with your subconscious mind.

Big brother is quite dumb

Your subconscious mind has no critical thinking skills and has no way to tell whether what you are telling him is in your interest or not. If you repeat something to your subconscious mind enough times, it will eventually believe it. That's why you have to be extremely careful about the way you talk to yourself. That's also why positive affirmations work. Be aware that your mind is constantly eavesdropping on your thoughts.

How to get rid of limiting beliefs

As mentioned previously, limiting beliefs are beliefs that you've accepted as true and don't help progress your life. They come from what your parents, your friends, your teachers or society has been telling you repeatedly. During your childhood, you accepted those beliefs as true either consciously or unconsciously. To overcome your limiting beliefs the first thing to do is to identify them.

Tips: Look at all the major areas of your life and ask yourself honestly how you have been doing. How is your financial situation? How are you relationships? What about your career? Your health? Take the areas where you are not completely satisfied and ask yourself why are you not getting the results you want? What is preventing you from achieving your goals in these areas? You are likely to have some limiting beliefs in these areas.

Identify your limiting beliefs

I would like to...but

If you are not satisfied with your current job for instance try the following: I would like to change my job but... What are all the reasons that popped into your mind? I would like to have a better job but

- I'm not smart enough
- I don't deserve to have a better job
- I don't have the right qualifications

Or I would like to find an amazing girlfriend but

- I don't have money
- That girl is too good/smart/beautiful for me
- Girls are always dating jerks

In certain cases it is necessary to dig deeper to uncover the real reason for that belief.

In order to do that, you can use the following technique: Ask yourself "If that's true, what will that mean to me?"

Here is an example extracted from "Life Coaching: A Cognitive Behavioral Approach" by Michael Neenan and Windy Dryden:

Jane was anxious about attending a party because she thought:

I won't get off with anyone

If that's true, what will that mean to me?

—> That I'll go home alone

If that's true, what will that mean to me?

—> No one fancies me

If that's true, what will that mean to me?

—> If no one fancies me, then I'll be all alone

If that's true, what will that mean about me?

—> That I'm undesirable (limiting belief)

What limiting beliefs are holding you back? Can you uncover them?

Deconstruct your beliefs

The next step you want to take is to deconstruct those beliefs little by little by realizing that they are not true. Start by checking whether your beliefs are really true all the time and in all situations.

Often, without being aware of it, we heavily distort reality. We look at our weaknesses and compare them to someone we know that has a lot of strengths in that specific area. Have you noticed how we tend to compare our weakest points directly to our friends' strongest points? It is totally biased and doesn't make any sense so stop comparing apples to oranges. Because of this pattern of thinking we start to believe that people around us are better off than we are. Jim is smarter than me, John is way more confident than me, Jerry is definitely better-looking than me… So what? Is it a fair comparison? It misses the most important point: you have no way to tell how happy they really are. And if they are happier than you, so what? What does it have to do with you? The way we constantly compare ourselves with others diminishes our self- esteem and clouds our judgment regarding our own great abilities and strengths.

In reality, we have far more to be proud of than we think we do. This is also why a great friend or parent is critical, they often remind us of our own unique strengths. You might think that you are not good enough for X, Y or Z but are you really not good enough all the time in absolutely all areas of your life? Maybe you think that you stink at math, how about science or history or baseball? Maybe you don't know much about politics but a lot about the technology or fashion industry. Ok so you're not the fastest runner, perhaps you make a killer lasagna. The cheetah doesn't look at the elephant and think *"wow I'm so small."* You can always come up with thousands of things you are good enough to do, stop focusing on the few that you find difficult. Your subconscious acquires new beliefs through repetition so here is one exercise you should do to leverage the power of your subconscious mind and change your beliefs.

- When you feel like you are not good enough, come up with all the reasons why you are good enough.
- Take a few minutes every day to remind yourself all the things you are good at (you might want to write them down).

Remember that whatever you choose to focus on in life, your subconscious mind will look for more of that. If you tell your subconscious mind all the things you are good at then it will start looking for more things that you are good at. It will progressively change your current perception of reality. Similarly, taking 5 minutes to focus on what you are grateful for in life will train your subconscious mind to focus on things to be grateful for.

Look for information that demonstrates your beliefs are false

Sometimes, a single piece of information can shake your beliefs and change your perception of reality. Maybe you believe that you are too old to realize some dream you have, then you meet someone who followed his passion and created a business in his sixties or seventies. Or maybe your relationship is not really fulfilling anymore and you say to yourself that, after 15 years of marriage, it is normal. But then, you see a documentary on TV showing couples married for 50 years and still completely in love. Suddenly you no longer accept your previous belief system entirely. You realize that it was not the true reality but only your self-constructed reality.

Be aware that even in today's world where access to information is easy - or maybe precisely because of the information overflow - many myths still endure.

To give you an example, when I experimented with vegetarianism for a month I read a few books and did some research online. I used to believe that if I were to become a vegetarian then I would lose weight but then I learned that some famous bodybuilders were actually vegans. It instantly shook my beliefs about vegetarianism or veganism. For further information here is a website that features vegan athletes.

One other example was when I came across a Ted Talk video by Dan Buettner « How To Live To Be 100+ » that shows footage of centenarian gardening or riding their bikes. It made me realize that it was possible to grow old while still remaining healthy and active and this realization gave me the motivation to eat healthier food.

Once you have identified a disempowering belief, look for any information you can find that will show you why you are wrong. Read all the books you can read, watch all the documentaries you can find and look for people who have what you want.

Surprisingly, most people don't take responsibility for their current situation and reject people who have what they want as outliers. They just lucky! Don't do that. Learn everything you can from them. Find what they are doing and emulate it.

The basic assumption upon which you should act in your life is: if other people can do it then I can as well.

2
YOU SHALL NOT LET YOUR THOUGHTS DEFINE WHO YOU ARE

> *If there were nothing but thought in you, you wouldn't even know you are thinking. You would be like a dreamer who doesn't know he is dreaming. You would be as identified with every thought as the dreamer is with every image in the dream.*
>
> — Eckhart Tolle, A New Earth

Decartes wrote *I think therefore I am* but is this really accurate?

If you have tried meditation before, you probably noticed how your mind is constantly thinking. Buddhist call our mind the monkey mind. Our thoughts are like a monkey that is relentlessly swinging through the trees. Are you aware of this voice that is always commenting on your life, and often negatively?

As I explained in the previous section, our mind is constantly eavesdropping on our thoughts. For that reason, we should be careful of the way we talk to ourselves internally. However, what shall we do about thoughts that are coming from our mind?

You are not your thoughts

The simple truth to realize and that most people aren't aware of is that we are not our thoughts. In reality, even today we still don't understand where our thoughts come from.

Intuitive readers claim that they can read their clients' minds or that thoughts are out there and that it is possible to tap into those thoughts. (Please see my article on *Lynn Robinson's Divine Intuition – Why You Should Listen To Your Inner Voice*).

David R. Hawkins in his book Power vs. Force wrote,

> *It is the vanity of the ego that claims thoughts as "mine". Genius, on the other hand, commonly attributes the source of creative leaps of awareness to that basis of all consciousness, which has traditionally been called Divinity.*

Even today, scientists are still trying to understand what thoughts really are.

One more thing you should also realize is that 90% or more of the thoughts you had today are the same ones you had yesterday. Your mind is running the same old thought patterns again and again. Needless to say that those thoughts are totally useless.

The bottom line is that we don't even know what thoughts are, so why should we accept every single one of our thoughts as the truth? We shouldn't let our thoughts determine who we are. If we constantly react to our negative self-talk sooner or later we will get depressed.

You are not your ego

You may have read some personal development books that tell you that you are the sum of your thoughts and from a certain perspective this is true. However, it only holds if you believe that you are your ego. If you have some understanding of enlightenment, you might know that reaching enlightenment requires letting go of your ego. What ego means here is not what we usually mean by ego. What we mean by ego here is basically your entire identity. Your ego is created by your thoughts - all those thoughts about the past or the future create your identity. They are what you call "your personal story." Your personal story is changing all the time though because you are constantly interpreting events that happen to you through your thinking process.

I'm not telling you that you should seek enlightenment today, but what I would like you to realize is simply that your ego is not the essence of who you really are. You don't have to identify yourself with any single thought or act on your thoughts as if they were the absolute truth. They are not!

Actually, all your problems come from your thoughts. Test this out right now: try to be depressed without thinking. It's going to be very difficult because your natural state, like other animals, is not in a state of depression but rather a state of joy. It's so important that it's worth repeating: you don't need to listen to your negative thoughts. Don't engage them and don't give them your attention, with nothing to hold on to you'll find that they start to disappear.

To learn more about the ego I encourage you to read *"What is the Ego?"* on my blog.

We can only live in the present

We can only live in the present. Of course you know this but have you really taken the time to think about what it really means?

The only thing that exists is now. Every time we think of the past or the future, the thinking occurs in the present—now. Your past does not exist anymore and thus cannot define who you really are unless you think of it in the present. And when you think of the past in the present, what you do is only recreate a memory of your subjective interpretation of a limited fragment of your past reality. How real is that! What about your future? Your future is just created through expectations.

Be careful that you don't need to cling to your "personal story." Work on progressively detaching yourself from it by focusing more on the present. Practice observing your thoughts and your emotions without identifying with them.

To learn more about enlightenment

If you are interested in learning more about enlightenment you might want to read:

- *The Power Of Now* by Eckhart Tolle
- *A New Earth* by Eckhart Tolle
- *Awareness* by Anthony De Mello
- *I Am That* by Sri Nisargadatta Maharaj (this book is more advanced so I recommend that you start with Eckhart Tolle books)

Also please take a look at my articles on Enlightenment:

- "Awareness" By Anthony De Mello – Time To Wake up!
- 8 Things You Should Know About Enlightened People

A simple exercise to realize what you are not

Try this simple exercise:

Stop thinking for a moment - even a few seconds is okay - now ask yourself: "Who am I?" Descartes said "I think therefore I am." If it is true, who am I when I don't think? Am I nothing? Stop thinking. Who do you think you are? You are that presence, that awareness you can sense.

For now just keep in mind that you don't have to let your thoughts define you. When you live in the present moment and stop thinking, the reality is that you still exist! Use this new perspective to lessen the power you give to the thoughts that are coming out of your mind.

How to better control your thoughts

If you want to start becoming the master of your mind rather than being enslaved by it, meditation and mindfulness are awesome tools. They will greatly help you become aware of your thoughts. Start bringing awareness into your daily life by observing yourself. Instead of being lost in your thoughts, try to be present when you wash dishes, take a shower or go for a walk. Here is what you can do to bring awareness in these moments:

- **Become aware of the thoughts that pop up** during the time you spend doing what you are doing. Don't get caught by your thoughts. Just observe them.
- **Become the witness of what you do.** Watch every movement you are doing. **Focus your attention on your body.** How do you feel in your body while doing your current activity? (It helps you become more aware of your body and prevent you from thinking. You cannot think and focus your attention on your body at the same time)

Meditation is a great way to boost mindfulness. When you meditate, you train yourself to acknowledge your thoughts and let go of them. After practicing meditation for a while, you will become better and better at spotting negative thoughts and will be able to better deal with them—and it is only one of the countless benefits of meditation. You will progressively become the master of your mind instead of being its slave.

Mindfulness has a lot of benefits and can even be more effective in reducing stress, unhappiness and procrastination than medicine or other popular treatments. Kelly McGonigal demonstrates in her book "The Willpower Instinct" how repeatedly being aware of any urge we have (smoking, drinking, checking email, etc.) and "surfing the urge"—that is to become aware of how we feel and how the urge is manifesting itself in our body—can effectively reduce non-productive cravings and desires. Generally speaking, staying in touch with our negative emotions and observing them *as if we were external observers* is more effective than trying to repress those emotions. This is a critical distinction, too often we try to repress such emotions only to find them rebounding ten times stronger.

How to deal with your thoughts

Do you know about the white bear experiment? When participants of an experiment were told not to think of a white bear, do you know what happened? Well of course they couldn't stop thinking about a white bear! In another experiment, participants who were told not to think about chocolate, ended up eating more chocolate than participants who were told to think about chocolate.

Instead of trying to suppress your thoughts or your emotions learn to accept them. The fact that you are having a thought is the reality, but this thought doesn't have to become *your* reality.

Every time you have a negative thought:

- Accept it
- Observe it as a scientist would (how does it manifest in our body? Which parts of your body are tensed? How does it make you feel?)
- Ask yourself if you can let go of that thought and consciously discard it

The more you accept your thoughts and stop trying to suppress them, the less power they will have over you.

Replace negative thoughts with positive thoughts

Ex: "I'm not good enough" Is it entirely true? Does it hold up in all situations?

- I'm good enough to make my friends happy
- I'm good enough to cook
- I'm good enough at my job
- I'm good enough to travel by myself

The point of this exercise, as seen previously, is to gradually deconstruct the limiting belief behind those thoughts by realizing that it is not true, or that it is true only in a few cases.

3
YOU SHALL BE CLEAR ON THE MEANING OF SUCCESS

 Success is not something you pursue, success is something you become.

— JIM ROHN

We all want to be successful and success is a recurrent theme in the media. However, have you taken the time to define what success really means to you? What kind of person do you want to become? Here is my personal definition of success:

Success is when you work on becoming the best you can become, do what you love and give your best contribution to the world.

What is your definition of success?

Success is...

Too often people seek fame, recognition and money just to realize after years of hard work that those goals don't bring them real fulfillment and often they are left feeling empty. You need to take time to determine what success means for you. Don't let society, the media, your family or your friends define it for you. Only you know what success means to you. Ask yourself *"How can I serve people while doing what I love?"* Think about what you can give, not about what you want to get. As the Bible says *"Give and it is all be given unto you."* (See *"Step 3: Identify Your Core Values–Who Are You?"* on my blog)

What is the meaning of life?

Generally, there are two types of thinking regarding the meaning of life

- We were all born with a specific purpose (this is called the Dharma in India)
- We have to give meaning to our life I like both ideas and I don't know which one is true but it doesn't really matter.

Main characteristics of a great life purpose

- **Timeless:** If you could use a time machine and go back in time or into the future, your life purpose would remain the same.
- **Universal:** If you were born in a different part of the world your purpose would still be the same.
- **Inspiring:** Your life purpose should be truly inspiring and allow you to unleash your full potential and experience a real sense of fulfillment. When your purpose really resonates within you, what you are doing doesn't really feel like work anymore.
- **Transcend your ego:** most of us work in order to make a living, to gain recognition or to feel accepted by society. A true life purpose should come from a place of love not fear. When you have a clear life purpose you don't act out of fear anymore (fear of not being good enough, not being worthy, not being smart enough...). Although we are unlikely to completely get rid of our ego, we should try to base our

actions from a place of love as much as we can which becomes possible when our ego is under control.

Powerful questions to ask yourself

Let me give you several ways that can help you identify your life purpose

How can I leverage my problems?

Think about how you can give meaning to your problems and challenges. Rather than complaining about a problem, it is often possible to take advantage of it by seeing the meaning it brings to your life. Take the Australian motivational speaker Nick Vucijic for instance. He was born with no arms or legs yet he found a way to be happy and give meaning to his life by sharing his story around the world and inspiring millions. Victor Frankl in his book "Man's Search For Meaning" observed the odd phenomenon during his time in a Nazi concentration camp where individuals that were physically very strong often died long before smaller, skinnier and weaker individuals simply because the smaller guy had found meaning to his suffering.

How can I get paid to do what I love?

What is it that you like to do?How can you find a way to make a living out of it? Did you know that the word "enthusiasm" means "god within." It is impossible to be very successful if you don't really love what you do. If you don't follow your passion, you won't be able to keep moving forward after multiple failures. Only a strong "why" will allow you to keep going despite the hardships. Having passion will lead to fulfillment, which is real success, not just money or fame.

How can I better serve?

How can you create more value for society? Stop thinking about what you can get from society. Think about what you want to give to society.

- If you had all the money and time in the world what would you do? What do you love so much that you'd pay to do it?
- Take a pen and a piece of paper and answer the following question: *"What is my life purpose?"* Don't overthink just write whatever comes into your mind. Keep doing it until the sentence you write makes you cry. (See Steve Pavlina's article *How To Discover Your Life Purpose in 20 Minutes*) Don't lose sight of the only thing that matters in life: being happy!

4
YOU SHALL BE THE CREATOR OF YOUR LIFE

> *If you don't design your own life plan, chances are you'll fall into someone else's plan. And guess what they have planned for you? Not much.*
>
> — Jim Rohn

You can be either the victim, or the creator of your life? Which one would you like to be? Many of us fail to realize one very important factor in life: everything is a matter of choice. You are responsible for all areas of your life.

Are you giving your power away?

Each time you fail to take responsibility in any area of your life, you give your power away to circumstances and people around you. Each time you play the victim you disempower yourself and limit your ability to change yourself and move forward. Not taking responsibility means that you refuse to acknowledge that you have at least some control over most of the things that happen to you. You refuse to look for possibilities to make your life better.

Taking responsibility is not easy

Taking responsibility is not always easy, because it requires that you tell yourself the truth, that you accept the fact that you may have done something wrong or that you could have done things differently. Emotionally speaking, blaming people or circumstances is much easier than looking within yourself for possible shortcomings and mistakes you might have made. For some reason it feels more natural to blame people or circumstances. Refusing to take responsibility and letting go of our control gives us a false sense of relief. It also protects our ego. It is always easier to blame others than to change.

However blaming others is a huge impediment to personal growth. You are unlikely to reach your goals in life if you cannot get rid of this habit and start acting as the creator of—rather than a player in—your life.

Commit to take responsibility for your life

Commit yourself to take full responsibility for your life even in situations where you don't really believe you are responsible. Taking extra responsibility ensures that you are not overlooking possibilities for growth and change in life and are fully empowering yourself.

Taking responsibility never means beating yourself up or blaming yourself. That kind of attitude is likely to be counterproductive and result in self-sabotage, leading you to give up and giving you further excuses not to change and move forward. Taking responsibility is accepting the reality and realizing you have at least some power to change it.

Am I responsible for absolutely everything?

I know you are thinking: what if something I have absolutely no control over happens to me? What if my husband or wife gets killed in a terrorist attack? I am responsible for that? While you are not responsible for this event you are responsible for the way you choose to react to it. You can find meaning from the tragedy and move forward with your life or you can live in the past, thinking all day long about ways to track the terrorist down and take your revenge. Revenge is a current theme of many movies and is appealing for a lot of people. However, revenge is an ego game and without a doubt one of the most destructive behaviors in the world. Revenge is the antithesis of peace of mind and cannot bring fulfillment. Martin Luther King once said,

Darkness cannot drive out darkness; only light can do that. Hate cannot drive out hate; only love can do that.

Unfortunately, too often our focus is on taking revenge, getting even or being right rather than on being happy. However, you should realize that in the end, the reason why you forgive people and move on is not because you are an extremely nice and completely selfless person, it is because you understand that it is the only way to be at peace with yourself. Forgiveness is nothing more than a declaration of love to yourself. It is a critical part of the commitment you made to yourself to be happy no matter what.

Events that happened to you happened to you, the question is *"what are you going to do about it?"* Are you going to let them ruin your life or are you going to build strength and meaning out of them—only you can decide.

I invite you to take some time to identify areas of your life where you are giving power away by refusing, consciously or unconsciously, to take full responsibility. Your family or your friends may support you in life but in the end you are always alone. The reality is that nobody is coming to save you. Nobody can get married for you and die for you. Don't live your life by default, create your life!

Some areas where you should take responsibility

Here are some areas where you should take responsibility:

- Accepting reality
- Your attitude
- Your happiness
- Your relationships
- Your emotions
- Your career
- Your time
- Saying no

Accepting the reality

You are responsible for accepting reality as it is. If your life sucks well then admit it to yourself. You have to be completely honest with yourself. No real change is possible before you accept reality. Now get real with yourself but don't make it worse than the situation actually is. The purpose isn't to depress yourself but rather to realize that awareness is the prerequisite for change.

Your attitude

> *It is hard to convince people sometimes that the world experience is the reflection of their attitude. They take the attitude that if people would only be nice to them they'd be nice in return. They are like the person sitting in the front of a cold stove, waiting for the heat. Until they put in the fuel, there ain't gonna be any heat. It is up to them to act first. It has to start somewhere. Let it begin with us.*
>
> — EARL NIGHTINGALE, LEAD THE FIELD

Working on your attitude is one of the most important things you can do for your personal growth. Most people when they leave their house in the morning have a neutral attitude. They don't choose their attitude. By not being aware of your attitude you give power to your environment. For instance, if you happen to be surrounded by cheerful people you will react to that cheerfulness and everything will be great. However, if you are surrounded by pessimistic people, you will easily be influenced by their negative attitude. By refusing to deliberately choose your attitude you disempower yourself, you become a chameleon that simply reacts to your environment. You are being influenced rather than influencing. You might say to yourself *"That person is not smiling at me. He is not friendly. Why should I be friendly with him?"* The problem with this is that that person might be thinking the exact same thing about you! Don't give your power away, choose your attitude and be the scriptwriter of your life not a chameleon reacting to life.

If other people insult you, make fun of you or disrespect you it is their problem not yours. Don't take anything personally. Realize that most people haven't done enough personal development work to master their emotions and are still acting at a low level of consciousness. Understand that they probably have their personal issues which explain why they are behaving like they are. And anyway they might judge you but what do they know about you? Nothing! You have nothing to gain by reacting. Do you value your happiness and your peace of mind or some criticism from someone who knows nothing about you? Don't give your power away by reacting. You are better than that.

Decide to leave home every morning with a great attitude Influence people by your positive attitude and don't let people influence you with their negative attitude. If people are angry, stressed or in a bad mood it is their problem not yours. Don't change your attitude. Do your best to react to people who are rude the same way you would react to people who are nice.

Remember:

Your attitude not your aptitude, will determine your altitude.

— – Zig Ziglar

Your happiness

 It is only when we assume responsibility for our happiness that we will have a reasonable chance of gaining it.

— Irvine, A Guide to the Good Life

I often hear people saying that happiness is subjective. Although it is true that what makes me happy might not make you happy, I believe that the mechanism that leads to happiness is the same for every human being and should be known by everyone.

Happiness: are we all equal?

Sonja Lyubomirsky's book "The How Of Happiness" shows that we all have a different baseline in terms of happiness. Some of us are born happier than others and, according to Sonja, roughly 50% of happiness is determined by genetics. The remaining 50% is divided as follows: 40% comes from what we do and how we think and 10% comes from life circumstances. The implication is that, what happens to us has very little impact on our happiness level. The only way we can significantly increase our happiness is by changing our thoughts and our actions. Happiness comes from within you not from outside of you.

Now we have all heard that happiness comes from within and that material things won't make us happy, but the question is: do you believe it? Have you ever thought about it seriously?

Let me ask you this: *Can you think about something that you were sure would make you happy once and then you finally it?* Did it really increase your happiness? How many minutes did the feeling of elation last? It didn't really transform your life as you had expected, right?

You probably believe that having more money or more recognition will bring you happiness. I'm also guilty of sharing the same flawed belief. I focus on my goals and tell myself that I need to achieve these goals in order to be fulfilled. I truly believe that the accomplishment of a particular goal will make me happy. However, when I take some time to think about my past accomplishments and how they contribute to my present happiness, I start becoming skeptical.

When I envision my future self having realized all of my goals I feel happy and excited, but at the same time, when I come back to earth and ask myself: *If right now all of my goals were accomplished, given my current mindset, would I be significantly happier than I'm now?*

Ask yourself that question too: *If you could achieve all your goals today, would it make you happier knowing your current mindset?* It might give you some comfort or satisfaction for a while, but is it going to transform your life and significantly contribute to your happiness? Probably not.

Does it mean that you shouldn't set goals at all? Of course not. But you should choose worthy goals to pursue. Goals should help you become the person you want to be rather than getting things you want to have. Setting ambitious goals is important because during the process that leads up to those goals you grow as a person.

Gratitude

Feeling grateful every day is a key way to increase our happiness. However it's not always easy to feel grateful. We know we should be grateful but we often don't feel it on a deeper level. The best way to feel more grateful is by practicing and getting into the habit of shifting your focus from what you don't have to what you have no matter how difficult your current situation may be.

What I personally do that works well for me is to make a list of 10 things I'm grateful for but here is the trick—while writing my list I listen to a great song I found on YouTube. It really helps stir the emotion of gratefulness and the simplicity of the lyrics are really powerful: "I'm so blessed, I'm grateful for all that I have"

Don't be grateful only for what you have in terms of material things, but also be grateful for your family, the freedom you have or the sense of security you experience every day (just to name a few). Remember that things that were given to you for free (your family, your friends, your brain, nature, freedom...) are far more valuable than any material things you can ever dream of acquiring. How much would you sell your freedom for? Your mother's love? Your arms? Take time to acknowledge how much you have to be grateful for.

Be grateful for who you are as a person. Focus on your qualities and look for more of those qualities every day. Look for new things to be grateful for daily. Walk around your place, look at everything you have, touch things and think of the benefits they provide you.

After a few weeks you will experience more happiness and will be able to progressively shift your thoughts from a sense of scarcity to a sense of abundance.

Remember, you are responsible for your happiness. No external success will bring you happiness or peace of mind no matter how successful you are.

Your relationships

There are two people in a relationship so when something goes wrong you always share of portion of the responsibility. Stop avoiding responsibility. Often, when you listen to a couple having an argument it always seems to be the fault of the other for some reason!

Example of things you are responsible for in a relationship:

1. Understanding women/men psychology.

You should study the psychology of women and men. Many arguments can be avoided by understanding some fundamental differences between men and women.

2. Nurture the relationship.

It is always shocking for me to see how in Japan many couples complain about their marriage while they are making no effort to nurture the relationship. Relationships are like everything else in life, they require effort.

3. Communicating clearly your needs and how you feel to your partner.

You are responsible for letting your partner know what you want and how you feel. By failing to do that on a consistent basis you are likely to build resentment towards your partner over time. Resentment accumulated over a long period of time is a relationship killer. Communicating openly with your partner about things that bother you in the relationship, even small things, is crucial. It is something I'm really struggling with and I know I have to seriously work on this aspect of my life. I expect women to know how I feel and what I want without clearly communicating my feelings. I focus too much on my partner's needs and not enough on myself and fail to communicate clearly my needs. Then I secretly resent her for not responding to my needs!

4. Being clear on your values and expectations.

It is your responsibility to know your values and to stand up for those values. Don't try to change your partner's values and don't try to change your values to adapt them to your partner's values. We are attracted to people who are similar to us and this is also true for values. If you practice meditation two hours every day and have no interest in material things you probably don't want to marry a very materialistic woman. A while ago, I was talking to a Japanese man who was very sad about the way is marriage was going. He told me he didn't communicate enough with his wife and he realized after a while that they didn't have the same values, they didn't want the same things in life. Don't let that happen to you! Be clear about your values and expectations and share them with your partner.

Your emotions

> *An emotion has a very short life span. It is like a momentary ripple or wave on the surface of your Being.*
>
> — ECKHART TOLLE, THE POWER OF NOW, A GUIDE TO SPIRITUAL ENLIGHTENMENT

Happiness, sadness, stress, hopelessness and any other possible kind of emotion that you feel doesn't actually exist out there. They are only created by your mind. You are responsible for your emotions so it's up to you to do something about your emotions. If you constantly think about bad events that happened to you in the past, you are responsible for that! If you constantly worry about the future, you are responsible for that too! If you react too emotionally to a present situation guess who's responsible? That's right, you are responsible. That's why many spiritual teachers stress the importance of:

- Living in the now (the only reality that exists)
- Acceptance (stop resisting and begin to fully accept reality)

Being responsible for your emotions doesn't mean that you are always full of joy and can completely get rid of your negative emotions, though it is a noble ideal that you should try to pursue. By accepting responsibility for your emotions you start improving your situation. If you realize that stress is not because of a specific situation but is the result of the way you yourself react to that situation you can start taking full responsibility for your stress and look for ways to reduce it. If a situation or a job is really too stressful for you to deal with, you can always choose to leave.

Similarly, getting angry doesn't have to be an automatic response to someone who insults you, disrespects you or makes fun of you. You always have a choice. Be aware that each time you react and get angry, or try to take revenge you're choosing to give your power away to the person who is offending you. You actually make that person more important than he or she is. You might feel a strong need to react. You might insult that person in return, be sarcastic, take revenge, badmouth him behind his back or even worse chose to fight him. However, you have absolutely nothing to gain by doing that. You are just wasting your time and your energy. Actually, those behaviors reveal how insecure you are inside no matter how confident you might pretend to be on the outside. A person with high self-esteem feels less need to be respected or approved of by others. What about you? How secure are you?

By the way, the Greek stoic philosopher Epictetus said,

> *What is insulting is not the person who abuses you or hits you, but the judgment about them that they are insulting. Another person will not do you harm unless you wish it.*

Having said that, it doesn't mean that you should never react. It is also important to speak up in a polite and non-aggressive way when needed. It is especially true if the person who is respecting you is someone you meet on a regular basis, at work for instance. You really don't want to feel any kind of resentment towards that person. So if you have something to say, please say it but don't spend any time being angry about what someone did to you when that person is not even around. While you are worrying he/she is probably enjoying life and likely does not even know that you are angry at them. Say what you have to say but always be a gentleman about it. Write an email or ask someone else to convey your feelings to that person if you need to.

We know when we are offended. We just feel it. We also know when we will feel some resentment if we don't speak up in a given situation.

For that reason, if right now you are someone who feels offended rather easily it is necessary that you speak up. However you will find that the more you work on yourself, learn to reframe situations, understand that you are too important to react to most of the situations and develop self-esteem the less you will feel offended. Trust your feelings and speak up to tell people how you feel when necessary. Don't insult, make sarcastic comments or try to take revenge!

What I personally do to deal with my anger

I acknowledge that I have a feeling of anger and focus on how anger feels in my body. Focusing on my emotions allows me to dissociate from them. Then I analyze why I am feeling that emotion.

I reframe the situation: This person has probably some problems in his life (he lost his job, he just broke up with his girlfriend, someone died in his family or maybe he is just a jerk). I transform my anger into pity and see them as weak for lacking self-control. Often, when people get angry at you, it is not personal. You just happen to be there at the wrong moment when they needed to let off some steam.

I see myself as too important to spend any time or energy reacting to people who don't deserve it. My peace of mind is too important.

If I feel somewhat offended I try to understand why? If someone criticizes you and you feel offended, generally it means that there is at least an ounce of truth in their message. Try to find it but be aware that it is not necessary an "objective truth." It could be something that your subconscious mind perceives as a truth. For instance, I tend to believe that no matter how hard I work it is never enough. So if someone I know were to come to me and criticize me by calling me lazy I would likely feel offended. Not because they are right because I am objectively working hard but because my subconscious mind ridiculously believes it to be true.

Your career

 When you accept complete responsibility for your life, you begin to view yourself as self-employed, no matter who signs your paycheck. You see yourself as the president of your own personal service corporation. You see yourself as an entrepreneur heading a company with one employee: you.

— BRIAN TRACY

You are responsible for creating more value for your company and for the society as a whole. You are responsible for making yourself more valuable by reading material in your field of expertise, constantly increasing your productivity, learning new skills, participating in training sessions or working on your communication skills. Your company might be very supportive but ultimately it is always your responsibility to grow.

Your time

 Being busy is a form of laziness – lazy thinking and indiscriminate action.

— TIM FERRIS

Are you controlling your time? Or are you letting situations and people steal your time?

Your life can be described as a very short period of time that you were given on earth. Your time is one of the most precious assets you have. Nevertheless, most people waste a lot of their time pursuing things just to realize that those things don't really matter.

You have to realize that you are always the one who decides how you should use your time. You should take full responsibility for it.

Saying no

Before accepting an invitation, or responding favorably to a request, you should always ask yourself, is it the best way for me to spend my time right now. Learn to say no especially when the request is not in line with your core values and things that really matter to you.

5

YOU SHALL SET GOALS

> *A goal is a dream with a deadline.*
>
> — Napoleon Hill

> *Nothing happens, no forward steps are taken until a goal is established. Without goals individuals just wander through life. They stumble along. Never knowing where they are going, so they never get anywhere.*
>
> — David J. Schwartz, The Magic Of Thinking Big

Have you defined clear goals in your life? Did you take the time to write down your goals? Setting goals and writing them down is probably one of the best gifts you can give yourself. It is the best way to tap into the power of your subconscious mind and let it support you. Setting goals provides you with a lot of other benefits and helps you clarify what you really want in life. However, surprisingly, few people go through the process of writing down their goals. That's exactly why I felt the need to write a book on goal setting (you can learn more about it at the end of this ebook). Goal setting is so powerful that I believe everyone should learn about it.

Here are 5 great reasons why you should set goals in your life:

1. It gives direction to your subconscious mind that Maxwell Maltz calls a mechanical goal-seeking device. Here is a quote from his book Psycho-cybernetics,

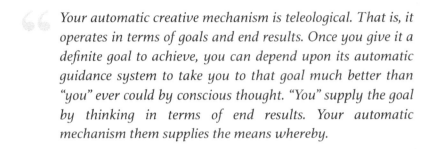

Your automatic creative mechanism is teleological. That is, it operates in terms of goals and end results. Once you give it a definite goal to achieve, you can depend upon its automatic guidance system to take you to that goal much better than "you" ever could by conscious thought. "You" supply the goal by thinking in terms of end results. Your automatic mechanism them supplies the means whereby.

2. It empowers you: when you set goals in all the areas of your life, you act as the creator of your life not the victim. You realize that you have the power within you to achieve goals that truly excite you and get you the life you deserve.

3. It contributes to building a healthy amount of self-esteem: achieving goals you set for yourself is a powerful way to build self-esteem. Start with small goals. The more goals that you achieve the more you will believe in your ability to achieve even greater goals and build an even healthier level of self-esteem.

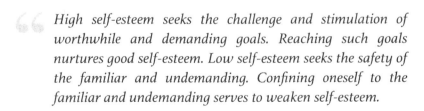

High self-esteem seeks the challenge and stimulation of worthwhile and demanding goals. Reaching such goals nurtures good self-esteem. Low self-esteem seeks the safety of the familiar and undemanding. Confining oneself to the familiar and undemanding serves to weaken self-esteem.

— NATHANIEL BRANDEN

4. It changes your present reality: it opens you up to new opportunity and makes you realize that you can overcome your limiting beliefs. You progressively become aware of the fact that your present reality can be changed.

> *The value of goals is not in the future they describe, but the change in perception of reality they foster.*
>
> — DAVID ALLEN, GETTING THINGS DONE

5. It improves your health: people who have truly exciting goals that give meaning to their life are healthier and can live longer. One of the 9 common characteristics of people who live to be one hundred years old, according to Dan Buettner the author of "Blue zone," is that they have a life purpose. Here is a powerful example: a mother who contracted cancer when her son was 2, decided that she would live to see her son graduate college. She went through many surgical operations, her cancer was never fully cured but she lived for 20 more years and saw her son graduate college before passing away six weeks afterward.

> *Use goals to live longer. No medicine in the world – and your physician will bear this out – is as powerful in bringing about life as is the desire to do something.*
>
> — DAVID J. SCHWATZ, THE MAGIC OF THINKING BIG

How to set goals you will achieve

> *The key to goal setting is for you to think on paper. Successful men and women think with a pen in their hands; unsuccessful people do not. – Brian Tracy*

The very first thing to do when you want to set some goals for yourself is to put them on paper. The mere act of writing down your goals will instantly make them more concrete in your mind. Putting goals on paper moves those goals that you enjoy daydreaming about from the abstract world to the physical world. Daydreaming is a trick that you might use to feel good right now but it is an illusion that rarely produces results. Once you take the time to write down your goals you'll find that they start becoming part of your reality.

Are you ready to set your goals? Take a piece of paper and pen and write down all the goals you would like to achieve if you were guaranteed to succeed no matter what.

Go for goals that really excite you even if they sound totally crazy to others. What is it that you really want? What would your dream life look like? What is your way to contribute to the world? Unleash your imagination.

Take the goal that excites you the most and ask you "*how*?" "*How can I achieve it*?" Questions that start with "How" are very powerful. They foster your imagination and are based on the assumption that whatever it is that you want to accomplish is possible. By brainstorming about your goal, you will progressively make it part of your reality and by chunking it down and choosing a realistic deadline and working at it daily you will start realizing that it is possible. Not easy but possible.

Be specific

 Know what you want. Clarity is power. And vague goals promote vague results. – Robin Sharma

The biggest mistake is to set goals that are vague like "*I'm going study English*" or "*I want to become rich.*" Your goal should be very clear. Clarity is the key.

Rather than simply deciding to study English you should choose what you want to be able to say in English by the end of the month/semester or year.

For instance: I will meet my American friend John during the last weekend of June and I will have 1-hour conversation with him about my experience traveling in Asia.

Rather than saying you want to make more money, decide the exact amount of money you want to earn and commit to a specific deadline. Ex: I will earn $10,000 per month by December 31st of next year.

Decide on the specific day you will achieve your goal. The clearer the better. Find a way to measure your goals because otherwise you cannot be held accountable and cannot track your results. When you find a way to measure your goals it will become suddenly more real, more tangible.

Choose a challenging goal

You want a goal that will push you out of your comfort zone and make you feel better once you achieve it. If the goal is too far beyond your reach then you will lose motivation and your self-esteem will suffer. Don't compare yourself to others. No matter how small the achievement, if you had to push yourself a little bit to achieve your goal it is a big success that you should celebrate. It might not be a big deal for others but it is for you. And you matter.

I'm a big supporter of ambitious goals, but they should be backed up with massive action in order to be achievable.

Write all the reasons why your goal is so important

 When the why get stronger the how get easier.

— JIM ROHN

Having a goal is like being on a cruise. You don't care that much about the destination but you definitely want to enjoy the journey.

Why is that goal so important for you? Make sure your goal truly matters to you and is not something you are doing just for your family, your friends or your colleagues. Intrinsic motivation is always better than extrinsic motivation. Make sure you don't spend years pursuing a goal that is not going to make you happy. Don't expect that once you achieve your goal you will be happy. Your goal should inspire you and the journey toward your goal be enjoyable.

Make the necessary preparations before starting your goal

> *If you would like to be thinner, spend all your time with skinny people. Have all your meals with skinny people*
>
> — Vasant Lad

You have limited willpower so save it as much as possible. Try to create a friendly and supportive environment that will help you achieve your goal. If you want to become a vegetarian then have a list of vegetarian recipes ready, fill you fridge with vegetables and fruits or join a vegetarian association before getting started. Research shows that the easier it is for you to grab a certain type of food, the more you will eat of it. I noticed that I often eat food that is on my desk without even being aware of it. Fortunately (and not by accident), the only food on my desk is a box containing nuts which are great for health.

Share your goals

If you want to lose 10 kilos it might be a good idea to make a public announcement at work in front of your colleagues and to tell all of your family members about your goal. You might also want to tell people you encounter that you are on a diet and you will lose 10 kilos by March 31st. If you don't feel confident enough to do that, it means that your goal might be too ambitious for you right now and or you don't really want to accomplish it. In that case, you might want to check whether your goal is achievable or not and modify it if necessary.

However, be aware that your goals may change over time as you acquire new knowledge and new perspectives. If you believe your goal is likely to change, make sure that telling everyone about your actual goal won't put too much pressure on you. If that goal is not relevant to you anymore, you should be able to drop it. Remember that goals are here to improve your present reality and help you get the life you want. A goal that doesn't meet that criterion should be dumped.

When talking about your goals, avoid using *I will try, I think, maybe* or *if it goes well*. Instead use *I will, when I achieve, I know I will or I definitely will*. The words you use contribute to your reality so use words that support your motivation to take action.

Anticipate all possible ways it can go wrong and create a strategy

The fastest way to succeed is to double your failure rate

— THOMAS WATSON

We tend to be overoptimistic regarding our ability to achieve a goal and underestimate the amount of work and time necessary to perform the required tasks. Ask yourself what things can happen that will prevent you from achieving your goals? If your goals are long-term goals, chances are that you will face multiple setbacks before you succeed.

In the past I had many goals but I didn't achieve most of them. One of the reasons was my lack of confidence. Other major issues were that I was overly optimistic and was not prepared mentally to face major setbacks. I would try to create a blog about Japan but would give up due to some technical difficulties I encountered or I would wait for everything to be perfect before launching the blog. Needless to say that this blog never got anywhere! I planned to make videos of my trips abroad and publish them and it never happened.

Once I understood that failure was actually part of the process and not an anomaly it helped me significantly to achieve my goals. Here is how I see setbacks or failures: setbacks are here to test you, to see how bad you want it. When you set a goal, you have to be clear not only about your goal but about what you are ready to go through to in order to achieve that goal. If you already made up your mind up that huge setbacks are likely to occur, you will be prepared to face them and be able to keep moving forward. You should already know how you're going to react to potential setbacks before they occur.

Avoid putting yourself in difficult situations

If your objective is to lose weight or to stop smoking for instance, you should avoid temptation. Identify all those situations where you are at risk, think of what caused you to fail in your previous attempts and see how you can avoid repeating such situations. Maybe you like to have a cigarette when you are drinking coffee, when you eat outside or when you are under stress. Identify those kinds of situations and come up with an effective strategy.

How to create a list of goals

When you create list of goals you want to make sure that you cover all the areas in your life. It should include your career, your health, your wealth, your relationships, your hobbies and other areas you can think of.

Here are the characteristics of a good list of goals:

- Covers all areas of your life
- Goals are all measurable and have a deadline
- The wording is positive. Don't use "not" or other negative words but use "I am" or "I will"
- Check your list every day to keep your goals fresh in your mind and to give a signal to your subconscious mind to focus on these specific goals

Should you achieve all your goals?

You might want to achieve all your goals, especially if you share them with everyone like I do but in reality you don't have to and you won't. I felt a lot of pressure when I first updated my goals on my website. I thought I should accomplish all of them no matter what and prove to my readers and to myself that I could do it. However, after a while, I realized that some of those goals weren't really exciting me or that they weren't my first priority. I also realized that marketing my blog required a lot of time. As a result, I decided to drop some of my goals in order to focus on things that matter the most for me: working on my blog, studying, and writing articles and books. Things cannot always go as planned, so you should be flexible enough to adapt your goals and to trust your feelings to decide which goals you should drop when necessary. Goals are here for one purpose and that is to help you.

CONCLUSION

Thank you very much for purchasing this book, I hope that it helps you in your quest for a happy and fulfilling life. I'm looking forward to seeing you soon on my website. Don't hesitate to leave a comment or question as I do my best to respond quickly and thoroughly.

Don't forget to join me on Facebook here I wish you the very best in our life.

Thibaut Meurisse Founder of whatispersonaldevelopment.org

I'm changing the world by helping you achieve your goals

Would you like to set and achieve exciting goals?

If you want to go further and are serious about setting exciting goals for yourself you can download my ebook on goal setting on Amazon: *Goal Setting: The Ultimate Guide To Achieving Life-Changing Goals.*

Should you buy this book? Below are some of the benefits you will receive

1. You'll get a **comprehensive method** that goes far beyond the SMART Method and other traditional goal-setting approaches.
2. You'll receive a **clear, step-by-step workbook** that follows the method presented in the book.
3. You'll learn the **best tips** and **exercises** from the foremost goal setting experts.

Learn more at:

http://amazon.com/author/thibautmeurisse

If you have any question regarding my goal setting ebook feel free to email me at

thibaut.meurisse@gmail.com

What do you think ?

I want to hear from you! Your thoughts and comments are important to me. If you enjoyed this book or found it useful **I'd be very grateful if you'd post a short review on Amazon**. Your support really does make a difference. I read all the reviews personally so that I can get your feedback and make this book even better.

Thanks again for your support!

OTHER BOOKS BY THE AUTHORS:

Goal Setting: The Ultimate Guide to Achieving Life-Changing Goals. (Free Workbook Included)

The One Goal: Master the Art of Goal Setting, Win Your Inner Battles, and Achieve Exceptional Results (Free Workbook Included)

Habits That Stick: The Ultimate Guide to Building Habits That Stick Once and For All (Free Workbook Included)

Wake Up Call: How To Take Control Of Your Morning And Transform Your Life (Free Workbook Included)

Productivity Beast: An Unconventional Guide to Getting Things Done (Free Workbook Included)

The Thriving Introvert: Embrace the Gift of Introversion and Live the Life You Were Meant to Live

ABOUT THE AUTHOR

THIBAUT MEURISSE

Thibaut Meurisse is a personal development blogger, author, and founder of whatispersonaldevelopment.org.

He has been featured on major personal development websites such as Lifehack, Goalcast, TinyBuddha, Addicted2Success, MotivationGrid or PickTheBrain.

Obsessed with self-improvement and fascinated by the power of the brain, his personal mission is to help people realize their full potential and reach higher levels of fulfillment and consciousness.

In love with foreign languages, he is French, writes in English, and has been living in Japan for the past 7 years.

Learn more about Thibaut at:

amazon.com/author/thibautmeurisse

whatispersonaldevelopment.org

thibaut.meurisse@gmail.com

Need some help to achieve your goals?

Hire me as a coach and I will help you achieve your goals.

More specifically we will work together to help you:

- Change your mindset and your habits
- Overcome limiting beliefs that are holding you back
- Build stronger self-esteem so that you believe in yourself and in your ability to achieve your goals
- Create an action plan and take consistent action towards your goals
- Discover your life purpose
- Stay on track with your goals long-term

To learn more contact me at

thibaut.meurisse@gmail.com

Looking forward to hearing from you soon.

Thibaut Meurisse

Made in the USA
Las Vegas, NV
06 December 2023

82194482R00042